BBC MUSIC GUIDES

Shostakovich Symphonies

HUGH OTTAWAY

BRITISH BROADCASTING CORPORATION

Some of this material has appeared before, either in *Tempo* or in booklets accompanying EMI records, but not always with quite the same emphasis. I have also drawn upon a number of radio talks given during the past fifteen years.

H.O.

The music examples from Symphonies Nos. 1, 8, 10, 13, 14 and 15 (Exx. 1–3, 16–21, 26–30) are reprinted by permission of Anglo-Soviet Music Press Ltd.

Published by the British Broadcasting Corporation
35 Marylebone High Street, London W1M 4AA
ISBN: 0 563 12772 4
First published 1978
Reprinted 1982
© Hugh Ottaway 1978

Printed in Great Britain by Spottiswoode Ballantyne Ltd.
Colchester and London

BBC MUSIC GUIDES

LUTON SIXTH FORM COLLEGE

This book is due for return on or before the last date shown above.

3123

BBC MUSIC GUIDES

Contents

To the members of the Fitzwilliam String Quartet – Christopher Rowland, Jonathan Sparey, Alan George, Ioan Davies – in warm appreciation.

We are against simplification of musical language; we are for that ideal simplicity which has been characteristic of all truly talented artists, which has borne witness not to their crudity, but, on the contrary, to the wealth of their spiritual world. There lies the source of true innovation. Our contemporaries will listen to such music and understand it, and that should be the aim of every composer.

Shostakovich (1958)

Introduction

More than half a century has passed since the young Dmitri Shostakovich (1906–75) astonished the musical world with his First Symphony. It was widely recognised that a major new talent had appeared, and the symphony soon entered the international repertory, which it has never left. Many musicians confidently predicted a brilliant creative future, but none, no matter how perceptive, could have foreseen the particular place in music that was Shostakovich's at the time of his death. For his development, far from being assessable purely in terms of the flowering of a talent, involved a personal response to immense external forces – social, political and cultural – many of which were not discernible in 1926. Arguably, Shostakovich's music is more closely bound up with the life of its time than that of any other composer of the same generation. If this is both a strength and a weakness, it is also an aspect that repeatedly caught the interest of the world at large – and won not a few to the music itself. All of which poses special problems for the critic.

In the journals of western Europe and America, Shostakovich has at different times been presented as a genius, a victim of the pressures of Soviet society, an heroic figure or a lackey of the regime. Only too often the man and his music have been viewed from the standpoint of the West's ideological warfare, with little sense of obligation to achieve a deeper understanding. This may well have been less marked during the last years of Shostakovich's life, partly because he was so widely respected by musicians and music-lovers alike, and partly because the fires of hatred were less vigorously fuelled than in the 1950s and 1960s. All the same, it is still uncommon to find the music approached in a way that reveals neither ideological prejudice nor a certain condescension in response to style and creative aims.

First, the man himself, his personality and temperament. All who met Shostakovich speak of his shyness, humility and nervous energy. Those who knew him well – his friend and biographer Dmitri Rabinovich, for instance – stress his kindness, warmth and zest for life, and perhaps most of all his inwardness.

I have frequently observed him; he is talking excitedly to his friends, telling them something about yesterday's concert, or, with still greater fervour, describing a recent football match, gesticulating excitedly and jumping up at times from his

7

seat. . . . And if you look into the eyes behind his big, horn-rimmed glasses you get the idea that actually only one little corner of his mind is present in the room, the rest of him is far, far away.[1]

A biographical commonplace, is it? An idealisation of the artist as dreamer and visionary? Not in this case, surely. Anyone at all acquainted with Shostakovich's music will recognise at once both the nervous excitement and the intense subjectivity. Taken together, these two qualities are capable of providing many insights into the *kind* of artist that we are considering.

Whatever else he may have been, Shostakovich was highly sensitive; his inner, imaginative life was intense to a degree, and therefore complex and often harrowing. The release of nervous energy was proportionately strong. He wrote not only quickly but with an immense inner drive. Often, it appears, he felt an irresistible compulsion to begin a work, or part of a work, and to see it through in one sustained bout of creative activity. We know, in considerable detail, that the *Leningrad* Symphony was undertaken in such a frame of mind; the Eighth Symphony was completed in about forty days, the Eighth String Quartet in three days. Shostakovich himself would not have pretended that his temperament was an unmixed blessing: his work is uneven and his struggle for self-mastery was hard and long.

Inseparable from that struggle is the climate of official (Party) criticism in which much of it, necessarily, was conducted. To disregard this aspect, and in particular the two big crises in 1936 and 1948, would be quite unreal, but so would an attempt, within the space available, to discuss it in depth. For present purposes, the inescapable questions are surely these: how did Shostakovich react to official criticism, and in what ways was his music affected? And perhaps the minimum prerequisite is also twofold: a readiness to acknowledge that something more is involved than individual freedom versus bureaucracy, and a recognition that Shostakovich was himself a 'child of the Revolution'. He was in fact just eleven, and already composing, when the Bolsheviks took control in Petrograd. Among his juvenilia, we are told, there was a Revolutionary Symphony and a Funeral March in Memoriam to the Fallen Heroes of the Revolution.[2] Ten years later he dedicated

[1] Dmitri Rabinovich, *Dmitri Shostakovich*, trans. Hanna (London, 1959).

[2] Ivan Martynov, *Dmitri Shostakovich: the Man and his Work* (2nd ed., New York, 1969).

his Second Symphony to the October Revolution, and in 1930 presented the Third as *First of May*: each of these culminates in a choral setting of a revolutionary poem. All the evidence shows that the young composer identified strongly with the new, revolutionary order in which he had come to manhood. Interestingly, though, it was not until many years later that Shostakovich became a member of the Communist Party. Far from resembling that mythical stereotype, Soviet Man, he remained an individual, but one whose commitment to a revolutionary socialism can hardly be questioned.

These observations bear particularly closely on Shostakovich's development as a symphonist. For the symphony is a public form; in the USSR it is a form expected to embody some identifiable human content, if not a specific programme, and this will be discussed both musically and ideologically. At least from the Fifth Symphony (1937) onwards, each of Shostakovich's symphonies has occasioned a great deal of public discussion, and in several instances the world at large has seen fit to join in. Among the fifteen there are different types of work, and yet all, in varying degrees, are felt to be in some sense programmatic. Four – Nos. 2, 3, 13 and 14 – use voices and words, and two – Nos. 11 and 12 – have objective programmes; of the remaining nine, all possess some point of design or expression that suggests an underlying programmatic idea, though not necessarily a comprehensive one. There are differences in scale and character, from the epic nature of Nos. 4, 8 and 11 to the relatively small Nos. 2, 3 and 9, and also differences in symphonic density. No. 14 is really an extended song-cycle, symphonic in designation only; it is also a masterpiece in its own right.

Shostakovich was a prolific composer – the Fifteenth Symphony is his Opus 141 – and to discuss one aspect of his work, more or less in isolation, is perhaps misguided. However, up to and including No. 10 (1953), the symphonies may be said to represent the main line of his development; but in the last twenty years or so the emphasis shifted to the string quartets, of which nine were written in that time. This does not mean that the later symphonies are unimportant, but it does necessitate rather more critical reference to works in other forms. The present discussion will take the symphonies in chronological sequence, sometimes individually, sometimes in groups prompted by the works themselves.

Symphony No. 1 in F minor

This is the work with which the 19-year-old Shostakovich graduated in 1925 from Steinberg's composition class at the Leningrad Conservatoire. (The first performance, in Leningrad, took place in the following year.) It is also his Opus 10 and represents the climax of several years of creative development. This is worth stressing, for the First Symphony is sometimes referred to as if it had come as a bolt from the blue, which is how it must have seemed to most musicians at the time. But in relation to the works that followed, the First is a peculiarly isolated achievement; not until the Fifth (1937) did Shostakovich write another symphony destined to enter the permanent repertory. This, too, should be borne in mind.

The First Symphony cannot be slickly categorised. So strong is its individuality that meaningful comparisons are hard to find. There is nothing in the least unusual about the grouping of the movements, and the basic plan of each, the finale excepted, is familiar enough; but the total expression is distinctive, vividly realised and memorable at every stage. In point of style, it may well be that the work is immature or rather obviously indebted to certain models: *Petrushka*, the more mercurial Prokofiev, Tchaikovsky's lyrical ardour, perhaps Scriabin in some of the more heated textures. What strikes the listener most, however, is not this or that stylistic influence but the genuinely personal quality of expression. Again, it may be possible to point out weaknesses in the structure, but the overriding impression is of four movements that come to life as a single, unified statement. Even some of the supposed weaknesses have a way of insisting that they are nothing of the sort. For instance, it has been said that the climaxes tend to come too quickly, or too early, and that 'the physical energy displayed [in the finale] is vastly in excess of the real nature of the material',[1] both of which may be valid criticisms – in theory. In practice, however, these features undoubtedly contribute to the feeling of youthful eagerness, nervous excitement and unease that this symphony so successfully communicates.

Consider for a moment the principal theme of the finale (Ex. 1): to see this and its repetitive, sequential extension (from fig. 6 – miniature score, p. 63) as a case of chronic short-windedness is to

[1] Norman Kay, *Shostakovich* (Oxford, 1971).

Ex.1

misread the situation. Notice the deliberate 'breathiness' of the semiquaver rests and the jostling semitones; notice, too, that Ex. 1 is an anxious, hectic paraphrase of elements from the *Lento* introduction to this movement. Also striking is the recurrence yet again of a thematic tendency (*x*) prominent in each movement. We meet it first in the symphony's opening bars, where it is similarly preceded by a little chromatic ascent:

Ex.2

Moreover, it seems certain that Shostakovich knowingly related Ex. 1 to the principal theme of his first *Allegro*, itself derived from Ex. 2:

Ex.3

Three points arise from this brief scrutiny of Ex. 1. The theme itself, far from being a purely local event, is rooted in the work's basic material; the interrelationship of Exx. 1, 2 and 3 hints at an important truth about the whole conception – the element of through-thematicism; and once we have grasped the latter, we hear the cryptic phrases of the introduction not only as fully a part of the first movement, which the composer is at pains to demonstrate, but as a thematic key to the entire symphony.

Everyone who has written about this symphony has been fascinated by the introduction and the possible influences behind it. Robert Layton[1] suggests Hindemith as the model, and he could well be right. But the manner of it recalls *Petrushka*, and later in the movement the same material brings reminders of *The Soldier's Tale*. As an expression of the young Shostakovich that we see in photographs – poker-faced, intent, needle-sharp – this music seems peculiarly authentic, and its realisation, particularly the chamber-musical textures, is prophetic of much that was to come.

Two other features of the opening movement are characteristic of the composer's later music: the excited combination of themes, however brief, in the development; and the way in which the movement returns reflectively to its origins. The second movement gives prominence to Shostakovich's recurring *moto perpetuo* vein, complete with the familiar rhythm of a quaver and two semiquavers: one specific pointer to the future is the lead back to the principal section at fig. 15, where a solo bassoon plays the main theme at half the original speed. In the heartfelt slow movement, and indeed elsewhere, one notices the important thematic role of the cellos and basses, and in the finale there is a foreshadowing of the crucial turning-point in the finale of the Fifth: the intimate contrasting theme (fig. 20) is preceded by a strident, impulsive version of itself, thrown up, it seems, by the sheer excitement of the music (fig. 18). The nature of this finale has more to do with growth than with pattern, which is likewise a pointer to the Fifth. Mention must also be made of the keen dramatic sense shown in the reintroduction, in inversion (timpani), of the reiterated six-note figure from the slow movement. Invariably Shostakovich's handling of such a move is superbly assured: some fine examples may be found in the later symphonies – see especially Nos. 8, 10 and 11.

[1] See Robert Simpson (ed.), *The Symphony*, vol. 2 (Harmondsworth, 1967).

Apart from the imaginative appeal of the musical material, the strength of the First Symphony is primarily a matter of thematic structure and dramatic effectiveness. One would not wish to underrate the grasp of symphonic activity and momentum, but this is hardly the most notable aspect of the work. To suggest otherwise would give a false perspective to Shostakovich's subsequent struggle for symphonic mastery.

The qualities that have endeared this symphony to music-lovers throughout the world have everything to do with the composer's youthfulness, which is communicated with an extraordinary vividness and apparent spontaneity. A young man's ardour, excitement and zest for life, and equally his anxiety and capacity for suffering, these are expressed with a persuasiveness that is fresh and alive. At the same time we are made aware of the wider world and the challenge it presents. In the linked third and fourth movements there is an almost Tchaikovsky-like emotional fervour – though not, I think, any surface 'reminiscence' – and Shostakovich's tragic sense emerges strongly. The rising, aspiring version of the six-note motive still spans a *minor* third: a significant image from a mind in which optimism and pessimism were indeed terrible twins (cf. the last twenty-seven pages of the Fourth). The symphony ends in the tonic major (F), but with a certain emotional ambiguity, the major-key feeling being countered repeatedly by a chord of A flat minor (from fig. 45), which is in fact the last *chord* we hear, though F major is felt to predominate.

From the 'Modernist' Years (Nos. 2–4)

Shostakovich himself was dissatisfied with the First Symphony, which he considered too traditional, and in a very real sense he may be said to have turned his back on it. On leaving the Conservatoire he became immersed in the artistic ferment of the time, of which Leningrad was the principal Russian centre. Many creeds flourished. Art and Revolution interacted in a variety of stimulating and contradictory ways. As in western Europe, the rising generation found the prospect of a break with tradition peculiarly attractive; anything new, be it futurism, constructivism or expressionism, was felt to have something to contribute in the fight against the Romantic, 'self-indulgent' culture of the old order. Some of the assumptions were naïve and superficial; but it was a time of vigorous creative activity in which theoretical work was less concerned with fundamentals than with promoting new ideas. Warnings that 'modernism' might not only de-romanticise, but also dehumanise, were generally dismissed as academic and reactionary.

Shostakovich was soon in the forefront of the modernist movement and was much influenced by his experience with the Young Workers' Theatre of Leningrad. His feeling for the theatre, already evident in the First Symphony, was central to his development during the next ten years. Martynov remarks that many of Shostakovich's innovations in the later 1920s may be related to new tendencies in the art of acting, and particularly to a reliance on gesture and movement divorced from a positive projection of emotion. As he rightly observes, 'renunciation of the emotional and psychological is a similar phenomenon in, and characteristic of, certain works of Shostakovich'.[1] Futurist and constructivist principles also played an important part in Shostakovich's search for a new musical language. One immediate consequence was the repression of an innate lyricism; the mode of address became more 'objective', more impersonal, and the use of arresting incongruities – melodic, harmonic, colouristic, and especially linear – did much to establish a radical presence. This was a modernism of primitive motor rhythms, unexpected turns and jumps in the melodic writing, non-functional harmony and counterpoint, and over all a theatrical spirit of burlesque.

The most extreme expressions of this aesthetic came early rather than late. The Second Symphony, Op. 14 (1927), or at least the purely orchestral part of it, is far more 'radical' than the Fourth; and it is *The Nose*, Op. 15 (1927–8), not the much-vilified *Lady Macbeth of Mtsensk*, Op. 29 (1930–2), that turns operatic conventions upside down and inside out, with a matching attention to purely musical shocks and dislocations. The overriding impression is of manner without substance. There is no doubt that a great talent is at work, but it is equally clear that a blind alley is being occupied, however brilliantly. The works written between 1929 and 1936 show an increasing effort, first to make the alley more accessible, and then to transform it into a highway.

[1] *Op. cit.*

In the Second Symphony, Shostakovich deliberately turned away from all inherited notions of symphonic form. Even the title, *To October, a Symphonic Dedication*, indicates a new departure: the title-page does not say 'Symphony No. 2', and the music proceeds episodically rather than organically. In particular, thematicism and development are avoided; the principal means of dramatic effect are the contrasting of instruments in widely separated registers and the favourite constructivist technique of 'horizontal counterpoint'. This last is curiously named: non-functional counterpoint would be more explicit. Essentially, whether a piling-up of in early Hindemith, Milhaud or Shostakovich, it consists of a piling-up of unco-ordinated parts to produce an arresting, if nebulous, texture. In the Second Symphony, about two-thirds of the 160 bars up to the entry of the chorus are conceived 'horizontally'. This music ranges from relatively simple passages in two or three parts to such complex textures as are evolved at the outset and in the approach to the principal climax. So far as Shostakovich's work is concerned, the latter stands as the *ne plus ultra* of this linear technique. Beginning with a solo violin (fig. 30), the passage acquires up to thirteen independent lines (woodwind and strings) which are run together in different states of keylessness to form a steadily mounting *crescendo*. As the climax is approached, the brass instruments enter, bringing consecutive minor seconds, three deep, on the horns and fruity *glissandi* from the first trombone: the futurist conception of 'the Art of Noises' is surely at work here, and it is no surprise when, a little later (fig. 69), as if summoning the chorus, a factory whistle is introduced – albeit for a single blast, which has an alternative scoring for horns and trombones. The climax itself is splendidly judged, and the *Meno mosso* that follows is vividly imagined and precisely realised, with two or three notable pointers to the world of the Fifth.

There is a striking difference, not only in style but in artistic outlook, between the experimental constructivism of the orchestral prologue and the realism of the choral writing. The poem, by Alexander Bezymensky, begins with the plight of the Russian workers on the eve of the Revolution:

> We marched, we asked for work and for bread,
> our hearts were gripped by sadness,
> the tall factory chimneys stretched towards the sky,

like feeble arms, unable to clench their fists.
The only fearful words
for our fate:
silence,
suffering,
oppression.[1]

It ends with an invocation to 'October, Communism and Lenin'. The wording throughout is simple and direct, and this quality is shared by Shostakovich's setting. The first entry of the voices, by the basses alone, seems to reach back to Mussorgsky and forward to the Thirteenth Symphony; here is something archetypally Russian, an inborn expression of suffering, which underlines the problem of means and ends, style and idea, that the work as a whole inescapably poses. For much of the orchestral writing is what Soviet ideologues were later to stigmatise as 'formalism' – i.e. arbitrary, non-expressive sound patterns. Shostakovich himself was to use the term 'abstract experimentation', which is much more precise. A sense of perspective is important here. Shostakovich was just twenty-one, and if ever there was a young composer in a situation that seemed to demand a complete break with the past, surely it was he. Moreover, he was surrounded by men rather older than himself, each of whom was fired by a similar innovationary zeal.

SYMPHONY NO. 3

Particularly influential was the brilliant composer-critic and theorist, Boris Asafiev, whose ideas and enthusiasm were reflected in the piano pieces called *Aphorisms* (1927) and also in *The Nose*, two works whose opus numbers place them immediately before and after the Second Symphony. It was Asafiev who described the Third Symphony as 'practically the only attempt to produce a symphony from the oratory of revolution, from the atmosphere and intonations of the orators', which suggests that the underlying idea may perhaps have been his. Not that the young Shostakovich lacked a will of his own, either in formulating new projects or in seeing them through. On the contrary, the Third Symphony, Op. 20 (1929), though more musical than the Second, leaves an impression of almost reckless self-assurance. The ideas go racing forward, in quick succession, and are obviously the invention of a

[1] Translated by Myron Morris.

sharp and eager mind. Continuity, of a sort, is provided by a number of figures embodying an upward leap – usually an octave or a tenth – and by the familiar rhythmic pattern

but in general there is still an avoidance of thematicism.

Designed on the same lines as the Second, i.e. as an extended orchestral 'prologue' and a choral culmination (May Day text by Kirsanov), the Third is likewise an attempt to establish a revolutionary style, but this time without recourse to the more extreme forms of 'abstract experimentation'. This reappraisal of method, and in particular of the practical limits of non-functionalism, gives the Third greater clarity and sense of purpose. Significant, too, is the predominance of scale-like or similarly conjunct melodic material. The new linear method of working has not been abandoned, but for the most part it is now used in relatively simple textures and with a high degree of rhythmic co-ordination. This can be seen in Ex. 4: the three lines proceed independently and yet together, and the identity of each is clearly defined by means of spacing and colour.

Ex.4

Sometimes, in one or more of the parts an *ostinato* or a reiterated chord will appear, and in ways such as these a very fluid situation is given a certain stability. The reiterated chords are often plain triads, thirds, or major seconds, beginning functionally and becoming non-functional, or vice versa. But tonal contradictions are essential to the style, even in the simplest of textures:

Ex.5

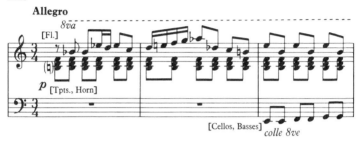

Although commonly considered 'less interesting' than the Second, the Third offers many insights into the language of the later symphonies: an important part of Shostakovich's mature melodic style is being formed – see Ex. 5 – as is his way of handling the orchestra to produce a sense of mounting excitement; repeatedly one notices elements of expression that proved to be of lasting value. As an achievement, however, the Third shares most of the weaknesses of the Second. There is a great deal of hectic activity and dramatic effect, which is rhetorical, but little dramatic structure; and the 'objective', impersonal manner still prevails, so that even the opening, said to be an evocation of a spring morning, is without lyrical rapture.

SYMPHONY NO. 4 IN C MINOR

Six years passed before Shostakovich wrote another symphony.

Indeed, the Fourth, Op. 43 (1935–6), may be regarded as the *first* true symphony that he had embarked on since leaving the Conservatoire. What prompted or occasioned this venture we do not know, but without a doubt the work represents a determined attempt to achieve a genuinely symphonic expression. It is possible that the motivation was a desire to show the traditionalists that a modernist, too, could engage in heroic symphonism: hence, perhaps, the largeness of scale and the very large orchestra.[1] But it is far more likely that Shostakovich's aim was to reconcile the (by then) most important features of his new musical language with the traditional concept of a symphony. This view is supported by the work itself and by Shostakovich's development over the preceding years.

Since it has often been asserted that the Fourth was 'in rehearsal' or 'on the eve of performance' when the official article, 'Confusion instead of Music', appeared in *Pravda* and changed the creative climate, a few facts and dates need to be emphasised. The Fourth was begun in September 1935 and completed in the following May. It was towards the end of January 1936, almost exactly halfway through this eight-month period of composition, that *Pravda* launched its attack on *The Lady Macbeth of Mtsensk* – and, indeed, on modernism in general – and it was not until the December that Shostakovich withdrew the Fourth while it was in rehearsal. Exactly twenty-five years later, during the Khrushchev era, the work was disinterred and played for the first time (Moscow, 30 December 1961). All of which leaves two big imponderables: the balance of musical and political factors in the decision to withdraw, and the extent of subsequent revision. Just eighteen months before his death, Shostakovich himself made these observations:

Having written my Fourth Symphony I found it too long. There were too many imperfect, ostentatious elements in it, the shape was wrong, the construction shallow, it seemed to me. I came back to it several times; I revised it over a number of years, and even now I don't think I've got it quite right.[2]

Beyond that the imponderables remain.

This is a purely orchestral symphony, in three movements, of

[1] The largest required by any Shostakovich symphony: quadruple woodwind, with the addition (non-doubling) of 2 piccolos, an E flat clarinet and a bass clarinet; 8 horns, 4 trumpets, 3 trombones, 2 tubas; 2 sets of timpani and a large percussion group; 2 harps and strings (up to 84 recommended).

[2] In *Music from the Flames,* a BBC television film produced by Ian Engelmann.

which the second is a comparatively short scherzo and the third a conflation of slow movement and finale. Some passages, particularly in the first movement, are on any normal reckoning greatly over-scored, but there is no doubt that the effect of physical assault is deliberate. (A useful comparison might be made with certain passages in the Fourth Symphony of Vaughan Williams and the First of Walton, both of which are exactly contemporary.) There are also many passages of highly selective, even delicate scoring, and in general the composer shows an impressive mastery of his orchestral means. The problems that arise have to do with the conception, not the realisation.

From the viewpoint of reconciliation, the long opening movement is full of interest – and of revealing ambiguity. On the one hand there is an active thematicism, including thematic development and transformation, a strong suggestion of subject-groups and a hide-and-seek relationship with sonata form; on the other, a many-sided non-functionalism, some arbitrary climaxes and changes in direction, and more than a whiff of 'abstract experimentation'. The more one gets to know this music, the greater one's awareness of the two worlds. Particularly striking is the closeness of the thematic working, though initially one's impression may be quite the opposite. Many have remarked on the apparent profusion of material, but in fact there are three main themes: (i) violins and brass, with accompanying (semi-functional) motor-rhythmic chords, immediately following the five introductory bars; (ii) strings, *p espressivo*, after the first climax (fig. 7); (iii) solo bassoon, almost unaccompanied, after two more *fff* climaxes (fig. 31). The first of these is shown in Ex. 6, the third in Ex. 7:

Ex.6

Allegretto poco moderato

Ex.7

These two themes are deployed in a number of guises, sometimes with their identities clearly proclaimed, sometimes more covertly. A good example of the latter is the hectic fugato in the development (strings, *Presto,* fig. 63), which is derived from the beginning of Ex. 6.

If the thematic working tends to be obscured or even half suppressed, still more equivocal is the form of this opening movement. Any suggestion of a conventional sonata design is conscientiously avoided, but the sonata *principle* is actively embraced. Formally speaking, the composer is having it both ways; and knowingly, I think, he makes a number of disruptions and displacements that confuse the form-making issue. At least three are of primary importance: the second theme, which is conventionally placed, is less important and less strongly characterised than the third (Ex. 7), which is introduced at an early stage in the development; throughout the more rhapsodic first part of the development there is little or no reference to material from the exposition; and in the somewhat compressed and delayed, but clearly-defined, recapitulation – complete with introductory flourish (fig. 92) and restoration of the home key (C minor) – the three themes appear in reverse order. A further interesting (confusing?) displacement in this recapitulation is the combination of the third theme, which now has a more 'masculine' character, with the motor rhythm associated with the first.

Why is it that both the thematic connections and the underlying form tend to be slow to reveal themselves? The main reason, I suggest, is the piecemeal, opportunist nature of so much that happens along the way: the transformation of Ex. 7 into a bizarre, 'heaving' episode for the two tubas (fig. 48) is one example; another is the string fugato already mentioned. There is no such weakness in the second movement, which is the shortest, the least heavily scored and the most convincingly shaped. A well-defined plan – *A-B-A-B-Coda* – is dramatically realised with an intensified return of *A* leading inevitably to a climactic resumption of *B*: a fine piece of organic composition. Ex. 8 shows the initial ideas from which *A* (*x*) and *B* (*y*) are developed.

Ex.8

There is really nothing else, and in each case the working is pervaded by a strong leading motive (*x* and *y*). When *A* returns, the quasi-fugal treatment produces some active counterpoint of a kind that is not to be found in the Second and Third Symphonies. The woodwind stretto that follows (fig. 139) generates a passage of 'liberated' semiquavers related in technique to the long *crescendo* in the Second (see p. 15). The difference is very striking, for these semiquavers are a natural outgrowth of the music preceding them and are felt to *promote* the return of *B*. The way in which this woodwind 'promotion' solidifies into a homophonic texture, carrying forward with the distinctive rhythm of Ex. 8 (b) an accumulated momentum, achieves a breadth beyond anything in the opening movement. The sense of tonal tension is also carried forward, the theme and its harmonisation being meaningfully at odds. This passage – and, indeed, the movement as a whole – shows a powerful symphonic grip.

A new influence in the Fourth is that of Mahler. Even the most sceptical listener cannot fail to be convinced of a Mahlerian presence in the slow march at the beginning of the finale. Hardly less striking, towards the close of the movement, is the 'fateful' image of a major third subsiding to the minor (fig. 249); in its doom-laden context this seems little short of an allusion to Mahler's Sixth. The march is the least volatile, and emotionally the most 'committed', of the principal themes so far. Not surprisingly, it is in the next few pages that Shostakovich's Fifth is most clearly foreshadowed; not only in feeling, but in texture and even in musical detail. The scope of this expression is enlarged by means of active semiquavers – already a prominent feature of Shostakovich's style – and by a forceful lift into C major (brass, fig. 159), which promotes a flaring climax that is again Shostakovich-Mahler.

Although at each successive stage uncomplicated and well directed, the finale is not an organic whole. The slow march (*Largo*) is an oblique introduction to a swift and incisive *Allegro*. In 3/4 and moving almost entirely in crotchets and quavers, this *Allegro* develops a momentum beyond that of any comparable passage in the first movement. Once again the symphonic grip is impressive, but there is also a fixation on a two-note figure which is a reminder of Shostakovich's earlier 'infatuation with unemotional constructivism' (Martynov). Having established these two very different expressions, the composer turns in a third direction, indulging his penchant for parody and burlesque. There can be no mistaking the impulse behind the bass clarinet and piccolo at the beginning of this section (fig. 191), and what follows is witty, engaging and delightfully scored: a harlequinade that is sometimes a waltz, sometimes a polka or galop. The deliberate grotesqueness that would at one time have figured prominently here is much muted and the overall effect is of a good-humoured gaiety, mock-naïve rather than sardonic.

How are these diverse elements to be brought together in a convincing conclusion to the whole symphony? The simple answer is that it cannot be done. Despite a persuasive transition,

Shostakovich's heroic peroration does not grow out of what has gone before; its effect depends on rhetorical assertion – only here, in contrast with the Third Symphony, there is substance as well as gesture. When this has made its impact, two strains from the *Largo* are reintroduced: the second strain, beginning with two rising fourths, is heard on the woodwind (fig. 242); then the first strain becomes the bass to a new trumpet theme (fig. 243). Suddenly the heroic striving ceases, and in an atmosphere of deepest gloom the idea with the rising fourths comes into its own. The whole of this closing section, from the beginning of the peroration, has a hugeness and an imaginative penetration that leave in doubt neither the composer's calibre nor his potential as a tragic artist. But as a symphonic resolution of all that has preceded it, this music is a magnificent *non sequitur*.

Far from being the climax of Shostakovich's modernism, as has often been alleged, the Fourth is clearly a transitional work. While there is much that is indebted to the constructivist viewpoint – and to the anti-Romantic movement in general – there is also a deeply human, Mahler-like expression that only partially succeeds in formulating itself. It is in the reality of this contradiction that a crisis may be discerned.

'*A Soviet Artist's Reply . . .*' (*Nos. 5 and 6*)

SYMPHONY NO. 5 IN D MINOR

It is well known that Shostakovich described his Fifth Symphony, Op. 47 (1937), as 'a Soviet artist's reply to just criticism'. How just? And how convinced a reply? These questions must not be left to the cynics. Indeed, a cynical view of the events of 1936–7 cannot begin to account for the quality and lasting importance of the Fifth. If we try to see beyond the vituperative language, it should not be hard to recognise that there was substance in some of the critical points, particularly those relating to shallow construction, lack of emotional depth and an unrelieved satirical tone. Moreover, to judge by his development over the preceding years,[1] which in

---

[1] See, for instance, the 24 Preludes for Piano, Op. 34 (1932–3), the Concerto for Piano, Trumpet and Strings, Op. 35 (1933), and the Sonata for Cello and Piano, Op. 40 (1934).

general was away from modernism, it seems likely that such criticism, however stunning its initial impact, found a natural sounding-board in Shostakovich's heart and mind. And if that is so, then he cannot have been unaware of the contradiction inherent in the Fourth Symphony. Precisely because his aim had been genuinely symphonic, the composer was confronted with a fundamental problem. What was needed was a more basic reappraisal, and it can hardly be doubted that, in the event, this was human as well as musical. He wrote:

The theme of my Fifth symphony is the making of a man. I saw man with all his experiences in the centre of the composition, which is lyrical in form from beginning to end. In the finale the tragically tense impulses of the earlier movements are resolved in optimism and joy of living.

Had Shostakovich's intention been *merely* to rehabilitate himself, he would surely have gone about it more simply and with greater certainty of achieving the desired response: by writing some suitable patriotic cantata, for instance. But he did in fact 'choose the line of greatest resistance, the only true line: that of fundamental, organic overcoming of his formalistic errors by an intense internal struggle'[1] – or, as I would put it, that of decisive re-engagement with the symphonic mainstream. An internal struggle? Possibly; but the Fifth was begun only four months after the withdrawal of the Fourth – and was completed in just three months. My own reading of the situation suggests eagerness and excitement no less than struggle. However that may be, Shostakovich was creating what has since become one of the foremost twentieth-century classics of the symphonic repertory.

The underlying programme is one of emotional and intellectual orientation. Although three out of the four movements (1, 3 and 4) are rich in expressive detail, the programme remains generalised, and the work as a whole is in the conflict-and-triumph, minor-to-major tradition of at least three other fifth symphonies – Beethoven's, Tchaikovsky's and Mahler's. As for identifiable influences, that of Mahler, already noted in the Fourth Symphony, is particularly evident in the opening movement, as is that of Tchaikovsky in the second and at the climax of the third; but the total expression is so strongly individual that the Fifth is still one of the principal reference points in Shostakovich's development.

[1] From an article by Georgy Khubov in *Sovetskaya Muzyka*, March 1938: quoted in Gerald Abraham, *Eight Soviet Composers* (Oxford, 1943).

This is a symphony in D minor, and it is not until the end of the finale that the tonic major is powerfully established. The opening movement – a *Moderato* that becomes an *Allegro* and then reverts – is a subjective drama, a conflict *within* the individual consciousness, worked out on sonata lines in a way that is at once complex, closely composed and supremely clear. Viewed against the background of the Fourth, the clarity of this expression is immensely impressive. Among the qualities that account for it are the simple but distinctive material, the absence of non-essentials, and the extent to which even tiny details have been felt organically in relation to the whole. This movement contains so much that is basic to Shostakovich's musical dramaturgy, as well as to his symphonic method, that a thorough grasp of it is bound to be rewarding. The composer himself returned to it when planning the first movement of his Eighth Symphony (see p. 38), and the first movement of the Tenth is similar in conception, the drama developing within a lyrical and contemplative frame. Particularly characteristic, in all three cases, is the 'brutalising' of themes, which is at once Mahler-like and pure Shostakovich.

This *Moderato* begins with great deliberation. There are four important elements in the initial statement (strings alone): (i) a challenging, canonic idea; (ii) a little descending sequence; (iii) a slow ta-ta-tum rhythm (once only); and (iv) a contemplative theme (Ex. 9):

Ex.9

In a lyrical expansion of this material new relationships are established and subsidiary ideas introduced. The principal theme of the second group is likewise given to the strings: the pace is a little quicker, there is a warm chordal accompaniment in the ta-ta-tum rhythm, and the theme itself (Ex. 10) moves calmly through wide intervals:

Ex.10

The onset of the development (fig. 17) brings a further quickening of pace and an ominous version of Ex. 9 on the lower notes of the horns. Clearly, there is a new current flowing, one that is to transform the material in an ever more agitated way. As the pace and the atmosphere steadily become more hectic, so lyrical ideas, or fragments of them, are combined, even fused together, in ways felt to be alien to their former nature. Ex. 11 is typical: a compression of Ex. 10, followed by a similarly agitated version of the 'descending sequence' motive:

Ex.11

This process culminates in a grotesque march – a travesty of Ex. 9 – and then the quickest pace is reached with a strenuous working of the canonic 'challenge' motive (woodwind and strings) together with the second-group theme (Ex. 10, brass), which is similarly in canon (fig. 32). The climactic resolution in D minor is superbly judged: a unison declamation (*Largamente*) of what was formerly (fig. 3) the most lyrical passage in the first group. Thus the end of the development and the beginning of the recapitulation are inseparably one. The follow-through is masterly, and in the recapitulation the events of the exposition are subtly reworked and compressed. The quiet, contemplative coda begins with an inversion of the first two bars of Ex. 9 (flute).

This description gives only the barest outline of the most deeply considered symphonic movement that Shostakovich had written so far.[1] Readers who decide to work at the score will find that they go on making new discoveries. Not that any detail, however small, is incapable of being heard. Nor is there any trace of opportunism – of mere manipulation, unfelt and inadequately motivated. After this very searching expression the second movement (*Allegretto* – A minor) is quite properly a relaxation: a genial, outward-looking scherzo and trio, formally unremarkable but well made, and in character and function comparable with the waltz movements in the symphonies of Tchaikovsky. For Shostakovich the achievement

---

[1] For some further pointers and a comparison with the Fourth Symphony, see Tim Souster, 'Shostakovich at the Crossroads', *Tempo*, Autumn number (78), 1966.

lay in writing such a movement without indulging in grotesqueness and eccentricity. There is a genuine gaiety here, and a sense of fun rather than satire; the ideas and their treatment are perfectly to scale, and the three-part design comes out in one.

Neither of the remaining movements can be described in terms of any standard form: growth rather than pattern is the guiding principle, but with a pattern-like use of contrast and return. The slow movement (*Largo* – F sharp minor) evolves from three main ideas, all of them meditative, and all capable of developing great vehemence and passion. Thus the emotional range is wide, and the principal climax is the most distraught, Tchaikovsky-like passage in the whole work. There is a distinctive fourth theme (flute and harp) which remains static, but its two appearances are vital to the balance and stability of the movement. Shostakovich's scoring may be said to emphasise the inwardness of this music. The brass instruments, including the horns, are silent throughout, and the strings are disposed in eight parts (3, 2, 2, 1).

The finale (*Allegro non troppo* – D minor) likewise demands of the listener an ability to retain and relate musical ideas, not a textbook knowledge of musical form. Curiously, this movement has received only scant attention from most annotators, some of whom have seemed to underrate it without a real understanding of its nature. Although the dramatic life is centred on the interaction of two contrasting themes, or thematic groups, this is in no sense a sonata-type movement, 'modified' or otherwise; rather is it a brilliant improvisation, spontaneous but well directed. (This improvisatory feeling is found in other Shostakovich finales – see, for instance, the Tenth and Eleventh Symphonies.) After the tranquil, even serene, ending of the *Largo*, the finale begins aggressively, and the initial march tune (brass) suggests a world that has still to be come to terms with. This coming to terms is what the movement is about, and the process revealed is one of considerable emotional and psychological subtlety. A second, rather quicker strain of the march music immediately follows on the strings:

Ex.12

From this material, especially the first strain, an extended paragraph is generated with growing excitement. A new theme is introduced climactically, as if thrown up by the sheer momentum of the music:

Ex.13

Allegro

Here spontaneity and long-term planning are at one, for by virtue of its two transformations, Ex. 13 proves crucial to the whole expression. The second transformation is a calm, lyrical utterance (horn) comparable in feeling with the second subject in the first movement; in the preceding bars (before fig. 112, horns and trombones) the rhythm of that subject is explicitly recalled. This in turn affects the character of the march. First the second strain (Ex. 12) is brought back in a massive augmentation, lyrical, reflective, *pianissimo* (fig. 119, violins): a fine imaginative stroke, but one that is easily missed, so greatly is the theme transformed. Then comes the first strain, also *pianissimo*, as if from afar, but still in D minor: no transformation here, except in presence, which is neither aggressive nor hectic. Soon the running semiquavers destined to play a vital part in the drive towards D major appear as a counter-melody. Shostakovich has been given little credit for his achievement at this stage; and yet the way in which the final climax impresses itself as both inevitable and striven for argues a high degree of mastery.

SYMPHONY NO. 6 IN B MINOR

The Sixth Symphony, Op. 54[1] (1939), also progresses optimistically from minor to major, but compared with the Fifth it is both less complex and more problematical. The unique design, consisting of a grave, intensely felt *Largo*, followed by two high-spirited *scherzando* movements, invites 'interpretation'. Both

---

[1] Not Op. 53 as stated in the published score. This error appears to have arisen at an early stage in the preparation of the score and has never been corrected.

Rabinovich and Martynov view the *Largo* as a 'calm, courageous and subsequent' reflection on the subjective problems at the heart of the Fifth, and the two remaining movements as joyful expressions of 'the liberated spirit'. Another Soviet interpretation, published as late as 1962, associates the *Largo* with the death of Lenin – solely, it appears, because Shostakovich had in 1938 planned to write a large-scale work in memory of Lenin! – and relates the second movement (*Allegro*) to 'the theme which is later developed in the Eighth and Tenth Symphonies, and the finale of the Piano Trio – the theme of "evil powers"' (G. Orlov). This is worth dwelling on, for two reasons: first, it confronts us with the tendency of Soviet critics to seek some concrete (extra-musical) rationale for the music they admire – and with the attendant hazards; secondly, the apparent contradiction between 'the liberated spirit' and 'the theme of "evil powers"' introduces the problem of tone, which in some of Shostakovich's scherzos cannot easily be brushed aside.

How did the composer himself view the Sixth? What was his creative aim? It seems likely that he was seeking to write a symphony as different as possible from the Fifth while remaining within the same broad orientation, both musically and philosophically. The differences are particularly marked at two levels: in the basic plan, as already noted, and in the musical working. In the Fifth, the progress of the music from point to point, though completely convincing in itself, often suggests that the composer may have been motivated, in some detail, by particular human emotions and situations. His own comment on the nature of the work (see p. 25) might be interpreted as supporting evidence, though not conclusively. The Sixth, however, gives the impression of being musically freer and more 'open', the invention taking its own course within broadly defined expressive fields. Thus the opening movement, for instance, seems to be an expression of Shostakovich's capacity for tragic emotion, and for inner aspiration, rather than of anything more concrete; in this it may be compared with the third and fourth movements of the First Symphony.

This opening movement is lyrical, to some extent contrapuntal, broadly conceived, and structured in two big sections, which are not so much recapitulated as brought back in *resumé* (from fig. 29) to close and complete the expression. Ex. 14 shows the two basic impulses:

30

Ex.14

and

In commenting on the initial material (Ex. 14a), Soviet critics seem fond of invoking J. S. Bach, largely, it appears, because of one or two intervals – the drop from B flat to C sharp (*x*), for instance – and the contrapuntal deployment. This opening theme is capable of appearing in different parts of the texture, with different continuations, and with its two salient features – as in Ex. 14(a) – in reverse order, but nowhere is there a high degree of contrapuntal manipulation. Melodic power, both lyrical and declamatory, is of the essence, and this is used spaciously with great certainty of effect. One interesting detail, in the light of the Tenth and Eleventh Symphonies especially, is the way in which the group of triplet quavers from the first two bars gives rise to a running, conjunct accompaniment on the lower strings (fig. 4): an ominous grandswell, capable of achieving both intensity and breadth. The beginning of the second section – solo cor anglais as in Ex. 14 (b) – and the climax preceding it are perhaps the most Mahler-like utterances to be found anywhere in Shostakovich's music. Nevertheless, the motive characterised by a shifting third – minor-major-minor – is strongly personalised and is an image of groping aspiration, however doom-laden, rather than of black despair. This motive becomes increasingly prominent, assumes various forms and prompts an extended arabesque for solo flute, *ppp*, with accompanying trills on the violas and cellos. This last, a point of work. There is also the practical point that Yevtushenko's poems are made as audible as possible. It is with the words that the music begins, in a very real sense. Shostakovich's response is both Mussorgsky-like and folk-like: the natural speech-inflexions give rise to lines that embody archetypal expressions from Russian folksong, lines in which the basic diatonic (or modal) intervals and conjunct motion are predominant. Thus the word-setting, for soloist and chorus alike, is always simple and invariably syllabic, and the manner of it gives immense scope to Shostakovich's mastery of diatonic forces. One immediate consequence is a thematic situation in which cross-references are felt to abound, sometimes through the working of a salient interval, phrase or rhythm, sometimes through a more overt transformation of theme.

In this thematic aspect, as well as in atmosphere, there is so much that brings to mind the epic nature of the Eleventh Symphony that one looks for an underlying 'motto' comparable with the Eleventh's minor and major thirds (Ex. 23). There is in fact something similar, though without the same commanding role:

Ex.26

A more fundamental affinity is with the eighteenth-century *buffo* tradition, which is not so much parodied as gaily emulated. The spirited invention is splendidly sustained, and the ending – more American than Russian, surely – is uproarious. This is an exhilarating piece, but those Soviet critics who find its gaiety 'reckless' have a point. For it is hard to feel that these three movements, each of which is highly imaginative, hold together as a dramatic unity.

Three Wartime Symphonies (*Nos. 7–9*)

The next three symphonies, very different from each other though they are, may usefully be grouped together. All three were written against the background of what the Russians call the Great Patriotic War, or Second German War, and it has long been clear that the traumas of those years had a greater impact on Shostakovich than anything in his previous experience. Whatever its imperfections, the Eighth Symphony will always have a place among those works of art in which the horror and agony of war are communicated with an almost unbearable vividness. The Seventh, too, is a work of lasting interest, not least for the light it throws on Shostakovich's development over the preceding years.

SYMPHONY NO. 7 IN C MAJOR

To wartime audiences the Seventh (*Leningrad*), Op. 60 (1941) spoke directly of the heroism, defiance and love of life of ordinary people. The first three movements were written under siege conditions as the Nazis starved and bombarded the city. Today, however, this symphony is seldom played – and often underrated. What is most remembered is the weakest part, the *Bolero*-like repetition of the War theme in the first movement. So strongly has this one passage embedded itself in listeners' memories that the whole work is sometimes referred to as if it were a grandiose battle piece, which is not at all the case. The programmatic element is very generalised and in the two middle movements seemingly negligible. The composer's words, as reported by Rabinovich, are a valuable guide:

(I) *Allegretto*. War breaks suddenly into our peaceful life. . . . The recapitulation
is a funeral march, a deeply tragic episode, a mass requiem. . . .

(II) *Moderato (poco allegretto)*. A lyrical *intermezzo* . . . no programme and fewer
'concrete facts' than [in] the first movement.

(III) *Adagio*. A pathetic *adagio* with drama in the middle episode.

(IV) *Allegro non troppo*. Victory, a beautiful life in the future.

Shostakovich was concerned primarily with the expression of
feelings, not the portrayal of events. Even of the first movement he
said: 'I did not intend to describe war in a naturalistic manner. . . .
I was trying to present the spirit and essence of those harsh events.'
The deepest theme of the *Leningrad*, determining much of its
musical character, is the composer's feeling of oneness with his
fellow-citizens:

I was guided by a great love for the man in the street . . . love for people who have
become the bulwark of culture, civilization and life. I have written my symphony
about them and others like them because I love them from the bottom of my heart.

Shostakovich was not given to that sort of comment on his work.
Normally he was reticent, even taciturn. On the Eighth and Tenth
Symphonies, for instance, he seems to have maintained a deeply-
motivated silence. In 1941, however, the compulsion to speak in
words as well as in music sprang from an overwhelming sense of
identification with the life about him. Surely it was just such an
experience that he had 'willed' at the end of the Fifth Symphony
and celebrated in the finale of the Sixth, but it was the siege of
Leningrad that made it a reality for him. Running right through
the *Leningrad* Symphony is an underlying joy, a peace of mind, as if
the composer's inner life had become simple and free. There are no
subjective problems, and in that sense this is one of the happiest of
works. Appropriately, the key is C major. A large orchestra is used;
not quite as large as for the Fourth Symphony, but with more
trumpets and trombones – six of each.

The question of the War theme – its suitability and treatment – is
part of a wider problem concerning the first movement. This is a
problem of form and content. It is already clear that this *Allegretto* is
the most programmatic movement, but the form that emerges is a
misplaced and misshapen sonata. The explanation seems to lie in a
change of plan. At first Shostakovich thought he would complete
the *Leningrad* in one movement, and with a choral conclusion, the
words of which he had virtually decided to write himself. This
suggests a dramatic but also episodic conception, comparable in
character, though not in style, with the Second and Third

34

Symphonies. The first movement undoubtedly reflects something of the original intention, and there is more than a suspicion that the recapitulation, despite its poetry and some deft touches, is a compromise between the programme and the need to complete a balanced design.

The exposition promises well. The first subject is confidently expanded in a way that brings to mind the finale of the Fifth; and the second subject, especially the subsidiary idea with the scalic descent, is a persuasive expression of heartfelt simplicity. Then comes the War theme, in lieu of a development. Programmatically, it is right that this should be new material; musically, organically, it is wrong that the new, instead of interacting with the old, simply goes its own way. The character of the theme itself is worth pondering. Remember how we first hear it: on plucked strings (*pp*),[1] accompanied only by the lightest of drum-taps. The tune is facile, jaunty, perhaps slightly cocky, but certainly not menacing. If Shostakovich really intended to portray Nazism on the march – it is often alleged that he did – he must have been dreaming of a paper tiger! His own words, however, were 'war breaks suddenly into our peaceful life'. At first it is distant and unreal – the jaunty flute and drum – but all the time it bears directly on more and more lives until at last the whole nation is involved in a life-and-death struggle. Gradually the tone becomes more menacing, the reality harsher, and a note of heroic defiance enters the music – quite specifically at fig. 45. The tune is not altogether inept for this conception, but its treatment is ill-judged. Arguably, it would have been wrong psychologically to 'develop' here; but is the over-simple reiteration musically right? Particularly questionable are those stages at which each phrase of the tune is imitated by other instruments. The dramatic resolution is impressive; it has breadth and thematic cogency and convincingly fuses the climax of the War episode with the beginning of the recapitulation. Shostakovich's description of the recapitulation (see above) is a trifle loose; there is no 'funeral march' as such, but the main theme from the second subject is recast as a forlorn *Adagio* in alternating measures of 3/4 and 4/4 (bassoon, accompanied by plucked strings and piano). This is hardly one of the more memorable of Shostakovich's transformations; it sounds contrived and falls short of the profound effect that we know was intended.

[1] Strictly, mixed *pizzicato* and *col legno*.

35

The two middle movements require little comment. Here there are no confused aims; the ideas are engaging, take their own musical course and are well stitched together: well stitched rather than organically woven. This distinction is certainly true of the second movement, which is indeed 'a lyrical *intermezzo*', but with a more vigorous, even martial, section at its centre. The opening theme with its predominantly stepwise motion is typical of Shostakovich in this relaxed, easy-going vein. No less characteristic, both here and in the second theme (oboe, with rhythmic accompaniment), is the vital presence of irregularity and unexpected inflections. Perhaps the most notable aspects of the slow movement are the almost ritualised opening with its somewhat Stravinsky-like wind sonorities and declamatory strings, and the wonderfully simple flute theme which follows. The dramatic middle section, though well integrated with the return of the opening, tends to seem intrusive rather than a convincing extension of the emotional range.

The finale is by no means the barn-storming type of movement that a vision of victory might seem to suggest. Beginning very quietly, it builds up gradually and deliberately in a manner owing something to the finale of the Fifth; the effect is both improvisatory and closely composed, and a sense of growing momentum is achieved from within. When at length this activity has been reduced to a single string line, there is a change to *Moderato* and to 3/4 and a marked change in atmosphere. Here Shostakovich treads a tightrope, seeking to avoid too great a loss of momentum but at the same time to give expression to a feeling of mass mourning. From this extensive paragraph the third and final phase emerges: a triumphal conclusion that uses the full orchestral resources and, just before the end, embraces the symphony's opening theme (brass). This theme gives an effective lift to the peroration, but it also reminds us that the material of the finale has less distinction.

Our verdict on the *Leningrad* today must surely be that it fails to achieve a profundity commensurate with its size and weight of sound. It seems likely that creative enthusiasm outstripped consideration; at the time Shostakovich was fearful that it might be so. And perhaps the very absence of subjective tensions tended to make for a shallower impact. Curiously, apart from the climax of the first movement, there is no fundamental opposition of conflicting forces: was there ever a less dialectical heroic

36

symphony? Here, then, is a possible clue to the work's declining fortunes in the past thirty years.

SYMPHONY NO. 8 IN C MINOR

As the popular appeal of the *Leningrad* fell away, so the Eighth Symphony, Op. 65 (1943), came to be more widely appreciated. Written at the height of the war, this symphony took much longer to become well known. The Eighth is one of Shostakovich's darkest and deepest expressions, and at the three-day conference on music presided over by Zhdanov in 1948 it was particularly stigmatised for its 'extreme subjectivism', 'unrelieved gloom' and 'wilful complexity'.[1] In the *Leningrad* the joyful release from subjective stresses made for simplicity, even over-simplicity. In the Eighth the creative drive came not from release but from renewed tension, which meant very different imaginative demands. In responding to those demands, Shostakovich showed what a great tragic artist experience had made him. There is no declared programme, but from the Mahler-like sequence of five movements and the nature of the musical content it is clear that a psychological programme, as distinct from a descriptive one, exists. Wilfred Owen's words – 'My subject is War, and the pity of War' – have an aptness here. For at the root of the Eighth is the problem of coming to grips, emotionally and philosophically, with violence and suffering on a catastrophic scale, and of trying to see beyond in a way that is neither utopian nor needlessly pessimistic. In 1941, comradeship and confidence in victory had seemed philosophy enough; but later the sense of human catastrophe – an experience that victory could not erase – made a positive, hopeful vision, at least of the orthodox, public kind, very difficult for Shostakovich to affirm. Hence the charge of ultra-individualism.

[1] A contribution from the composer Belyi is worth quoting: 'The Eighth Symphony was ignored by the press. But it was clear that this symphony had created both an overwhelming and a repulsive impression: Shostakovich had fallen victim to his ultra-individualist conception of life. The tragic experiences and sufferings that Hitlerism had caused mankind had captured Shostakovich's consciousness in an extraordinary degree. . . . The naturalism of this music, expressing terrible visions, creates a fearful, almost catastrophic impression. But the whole conception is one-sided, and dwells far too much on the dark and fearful aspects of reality.' (See Alexander Werth, *Musical Uproar in Moscow*, London, 1949.) This reaction is worthy of consideration, for it is honest, based on principle and by no means unresponsive.

The opening movement (*Adagio – Allegro non troppo – Adagio*) is modelled very closely on that of the Fifth Symphony. A comparative study reveals a marked similarity, not only in basic conception, ground-plan and proportions, but also in the material and its treatment. Consider, for instance, the initial 'challenge' idea – not canonic, but similarly distributed between lower and upper strings – the wanly contemplative theme that follows on the first violins, and the rather quicker, and warmer, second subject (strings) with chordal accompaniment. In the development all the material is savagely brutalised, very much as in the Fifth, only more so; there is even a grotesque, march-like parody of the contemplative theme (brass) to promote the climax: the original and the parody are shown in Ex. 16.[1] Apart from the greater tautness and intensity of the Eighth, perhaps the main differences are in the sudden change to *Allegro* in the development – a tricky moment for the conductor, incidentally – and in the closing bars, where a beautifully handled lift into C major may be said to foreshadow the ending of the symphony.

Ex.16

[1] Should we attach importance to the fact that, rhythmically altered, the first four notes (*x*) become the beginning of the War theme in the *Leningrad* Symphony? I rather doubt it.

The relationship between these two first movements has no parallel elsewhere in Shostakovich's work. How did it come about? The most likely explanation would seem to be human as much as musical. The first movement of the Fifth is a subjective drama, a conflict *within* the individual consciousness; it is Shostakovich at his most Hamlet-like. The experience embodied in the Eighth plunged him again into just such a vortex of anxious, complex questioning. This is a tragic work, and its tragedy is that of the highly sensitive, imaginative individual – the composer himself – no less than that of the millions killed or mutilated in the war. Such an explanation, though speculative, is at one with the immense and lasting impact of the war on Shostakovich's heart and mind.

The opening 'challenge' is a kind of motto for the whole work; a paraphrase of it, awesome and majestic, crowns the development in the first movement and breaks in again in the finale. Moreover, beneath the surface this material has a pervasive influence, conditioning much of the musical imagery. The opening figure – C, B flat, C – turned upside down – C, D, C – is the last thing we hear at the end of the symphony and is in fact the germ from which the finale has grown. (See also the first three notes of Ex. 16a.) The second movement, too, may be said to have its origin in a figure from the 'challenge'. Another interesting comparison prompted by the first movement concerns the cor anglais solo early in the recapitulation. In placing and in expression, this passage is comparable with the bassoon solo in the *Leningrad* but is much more memorable.

The second movement (*Allegretto*) is an aggressive march-cum-scherzo, and the same might be said of the third movement (*Allegro non troppo*). Each of these uses imagery drawn from the military march, and yet the two musical characters are quite distinct, the one being human, even in its ferocity, the other suggestive of relentless automata. The sequence is right psychologically, a sense of vitality and exhilaration giving way to an expression that denies all humanity. The *Allegretto* is propelled with a rhythmic emphasis and weight of tone reminiscent of the *Allegro* in the first movement. There is a deliberate coarseness of texture with multiple octave doublings of melodic ideas set against heavily scored reiterated chords. The chords are only partially functional, the melodic material being much given to steps of a semitone: Ex. 17, for instance, is harmonised throughout with A minor triads.

Ex.17

Thus one of Shostakovich's earlier techniques achieves a well-defined expressive function.

The *Allegro non troppo* is a remarkably simple and powerful embodiment of all that is meant by a war *machine*. There are no themes; the only elements are a cold, mechanical rhythm in even crotchets (initially violas) and piercing interjections from the woodwind. There is no question of anything being constructively developed; all that accrues is weight of tone and dynamic emphasis. This is the movement particularly seized on by those Soviet critics who complain of 'naturalism': i.e. an imitation of the sounds of war. In fact, however, this music is highly stylised; it deals in images rather than descriptive imitation. Perhaps the central contrast is the nearest approach to conventional 'battle music': a fearsome, bugle-call idea, again extremely simple and direct, but also individualised and memorable. When the 'machine' returns, the symphony is driven to the first of its two crucial turning-points, the beginning of the fourth movement (*Largo*), which follows climactically, without a break.

This climax is one of the supreme expressions of Shostakovich's dramatic sense, and as so often at such moments the means employed are seemingly simple: the mechanical, non-thematic idea is raised to its highest pitch of intensity, only to be banished by the authority of a theme that has everything the situation demands – nobility, breadth, a high degree of organisation, and connections with earlier material. When we first hear it, this theme rings out like an impassioned protest, but its essential character is grave, absorbed, elegiac (Ex. 18). It functions as a ground bass – there are twelve repetitions – but, uniquely, little distinctive material is developed above it. Instead there are

Ex.18

various sympathetic commentaries, mainly in terms of the theme's most characteristic intervals, the minor second and minor third. The effect is to throw the maximum emphasis on to the theme itself, which in this grief-laden context is surely a master-stroke. There are two main connections with earlier material: Ex. 18 both carries forward the rhythm of the interjections in the previous movement and renews the rhythm of the contemplative theme in the first movement – see Ex. 16 (a). This connection with the first movement is strengthened by a number of less obvious relationships, not only with the contemplative theme but with other material. Thus the grief and desolation of the *Largo* are closely related, melodically as well as rhythmically, to the problem posed in the first movement – and the dramatic plot, so to speak, is intensified.

Now comes the second crucial turning-point, and this, too, involves a linking of movements. The *Largo* is in G sharp minor with the leading-note (F double-sharp) prominently placed as a pivot at the end of the nine-bar theme (Ex. 18). Treat F double-sharp as G natural, the dominant of C, and you can be in C major at a stroke! In the context of a large-scale dramatic work, however, this is the sort of stroke that only a great master of tonality really knows how to use. When he makes this move at the end of the twelfth, and last, rotation of the theme, Shostakovich persuades us that it is at once the most natural and the least expected of outcomes. The sense of being lifted into clear air is strengthened by the simple diatonic melody played by a bassoon.

Nonetheless, this concluding *Allegretto* is emotionally the most problematical part of the symphony, for the tone is sometimes ambiguous, even contradictory – perhaps deliberately so. Clearly, Shostakovich had no intention of aiming at the kind of public, triumphal conclusion found in the *Leningrad*. The final pages of these two symphonies could hardly be more different, that of the

Eighth presenting a hushed, almost dreamlike reflection on the beginning of the bassoon melody – the notes C, D, C. The closing bars are marked *morendo*, the mood is totally absorbed, and the sense of assurance comes entirely from within. Here, perhaps, is the essential clue to the composer's meaning. What arises phoenix-like from the ashes of the *Largo* is not the will to victory or any other straightforward, collective emotion; rather is it the individual human spirit, and this is exposed to many checks and uncertainties. Despite the calm composure of the close, the affirmations of this movement are knowingly provisional (cf. the finale of the Tenth Symphony – see p. 48). Musically, there are few problems, though one goes on noticing fresh details. The manner is both improvisatory and closely knit, and the expression abounds in personal fingerprints. There are three main themes, associated respectively with bassoon, cellos and bass clarinet. After the harrowing climax, which is an enlargement on the peak of the first movement, the themes are redeployed in reverse order. The resumption of the bass clarinet theme (Ex. 19) in the immediate wake of the climax highlights the whimsical, poker-faced character of the theme itself – a classic example of its kind – and also provides a possible insight into the vexed relationship between this symphony and its successor.

Ex.19

42

In 1945 a big symphonic celebration of victory was widely expected of Shostakovich, and not only within the USSR. It appears that he did begin such a work, twice, and at each attempt abandoned it.[1] The symphony we know as the Ninth, Op. 70, written quickly in the summer of 1945, proved a very different conception, and its seeming frivolity much perplexed Russian audiences. Rabinovich puts forward a somewhat complicated psychological programme which relates the Ninth positively to its two wartime predecessors. He argues strongly and with apparent authority, but hardly convincingly. His argument turns on a contradictory use of musical imagery, which demands of the listener a peculiarly knowing kind of perception. It seems unlikely. Surely the Ninth is the least programmatic of Shostakovich's symphonies and represents a deliberate turning-away from the big issues, an attempt to relax into a simple enjoyment of musical sound – rather as Prokofiev had done in his Classical Symphony – but with the experiences embodied in the Eighth as the inescapable background. The simplicity, however, is quite different from that of the *Leningrad*. There is little here to suggest 'peace of mind', but much that is coloured by an underlying tension, only partially concealed by the gay and witty inventiveness.

As in the Eighth, there are five movements, with the last three played without a break. This is not really a point of similarity; the fourth movement, though of special interest, is scarcely more than an introduction to the finale, and in general character the work is Shostakovich's closest approach to the eighteenth-century classical symphony. The opening movement has been compared with Haydn – there is even a repeat sign with first- and second-time bars at the end of the exposition – and the *buffo* finale has a principal theme that amusingly recalls Rossini.[2] Many passages are scored for strings or wind alone, or for a modest mixture of the two, and even the fullest pages – for instance, at the climax of the finale (fig. 94) – do not approach the density associated with the biggest moments in the *Leningrad* and the Eighth – or, indeed, in the Tenth and Eleventh. The listener's impression is of a comparatively small orchestra, but for many concerts the requirements would be

[1] See Rabinovich, *Op. cit.*, p. 97.

[2] Invariably the composer most suggested by Shostakovich's orchestral writing in this vein. In the string quartets one is more likely to think of Haydn or Mozart.

reckoned normal: double woodwind, plus piccolo (non-doubling); four horns, two trumpets, three trombones and tuba; timpani and basic percussion; strings. It is surprising to see that the score prescribes up to 84 strings, including 10–14 double-basses. This seems at odds with the nature of the music, but it helps to explain why a typical Russian performance sounds weightier and less satirical than western European or American listeners have come to expect.

The opening movement is a neatly structured sonata *Allegro* 'penetrated by a single carefree and happy mood' (Martynov). A bright diatonic impulse is enlivened by a good deal of nimble chromatic side-stepping both familiar and wholly typical. The second subject is a choice example of musical humour – of a kind that Nielsen would have enjoyed, for it depends entirely on a contrast of instrumental characters: the portentous trombone and the skittish piccolo. This is close to the world of Prokofiev's *Lieutenant Kijé* and prompts the thought that several features of this movement might be construed as genial parodies of military music.

Martynov, who was writing *before* the upheaval of 1948, is straightforward in his responses to this symphony.[1] His appraisal of the elegiac slow movement (*Moderato*) is particularly acute, for he emphasises both the individuality and the rareness of the gifts informing it. What is involved is something more than the gift of being simple; it is the ability to reconcile simplicity with depth and subtlety of expression. Commenting on the main theme (clarinet), Martynov draws attention to 'a whole row of finest intonational details which would seem to disturb the diatonic principle of its construction, but which in reality are extraordinarily organic . . .'. This was not so much a new discovery for Shostakovich as a new formulation of unprecedented clarity, economy and breadth. Other important aspects are the chamber-musical textures and, towards the end, the interplay of minor and major harmonies. This last, together with the quiet emphasis on salient turns of phrase (especially from fig. 46 to the end), takes us close to the Tenth Symphony, as indeed does the finely-controlled feeling for line.

In the scherzo (*Presto*) all is gay and energetic again. There is some affinity with the scherzo of the Sixth, but the invention is both simpler and clearer in tone. The fourth movement (*Largo*), short as it is, introduces an epic strain, sombre and seemingly retrospective,

[1] *Op. cit.*, pp. 147–53.

and the mood is deepened by a recitative-like expression (bassoon):
the effect is out of all proportion to the duration, and when the
bassoon leads suddenly into the burlesque finale (*Allegretto*), there
may well be a sense of emotional shock. The further the finale goes,
the stronger the spirit of burlesque becomes. Some Soviet critics
have reacted very sharply to this vein, pronouncing it 'grotesque'
and 'a mockery of the listener'; British listeners have been known to
find it 'cynical' and 'disillusioned'. Such responses are too
widespread to be without significance. They tell us something
about the nature of the object. Subjectively, however, the content is
not cynicism but a high degree of nervous excitement and unease.
Perhaps Shostakovich's most successful finale in this vein – the one
least likely to be misunderstood – is that of the First Violin
Concerto.

Symphony No. 10 in E minor

Between the Ninth and Tenth Symphonies there was a gap of eight
years. Although in part occasioned by a deepening interest in the
string quartet – Nos. 3–5 date from those years – this gap was
mainly the result of the upheavals of 1948, when Soviet symphonies
in general and Shostakovich's in particular were harshly attacked
by the Party, in the person of Zhdanov, and by the light music
lobby which to a large extent gained control. Basically, the issues
were the same as in 1936 – the role of the composer, his creative
philosophy and the popular appeal of his work – but the
denunciations, and categorisations, were more crudely sweeping[1]
and the pressures to conform unequivocal. Shostakovich's creative
reaction was to withhold his First Violin Concerto and to write no
further symphony during Stalin's lifetime.

The Tenth was written quickly in the summer and autumn of
1953. In the traditional four-movement form, this Symphony in E
minor, Op. 93, is widely regarded as the finest in the series. There
are strong grounds for such an assessment, the means and ends
being superbly adjusted throughout; and the importance of the

[1] This was officially recognised in the rectifying resolution of the Communist
Party Central Committee of 28 May 1958: see the *Anglo-Soviet Journal*, Autumn
1958, which also contains an important article by Shostakovich.

work is underlined by the feeling that here is both the culmination of the wartime trilogy and a renewal of the quest represented by the Fifth. Many of Shostakovich's symphonic methods and modes of thought are raised to their highest level, and the vision is comprehensive and profound. There is a great richness and variety of musical images, and yet the basic material is simple and direct. Whether intentionally or otherwise, the first three movements begin with the same three-note figure, which in each case is a primary motive (x in Ex. 20). At the very least, this is symbolical of the oneness of conception that the listener experiences.

Ex.20

Soviet admirers were quick to remark on the resemblance between Shostakovich's opening (Ex. 20a) and that of Liszt's *Faust Symphony*: according to Rabinovich, an intended and meaningful association of ideas. The opening of the Fifth, too, had been considered Faust-like.

The large-scale first movement is another *Moderato* with a

slightly quicker second group –cf. the Fifth –but without a further quickening during the development. Although there is no question of the Fifth having provided a model, as in the first movement of the Eighth, there are certainly some similar features: the development of drama in a lyrical and contemplative setting, the dramatic 'brutalising' of themes, the resolution (fig. 44) in a forceful, declamatory version of the most lyrical theme (fig. 5) – these rather than specific details. A sure indication of a deeper mastery is the combination of less material and greater breadth. There is immediate evidence in the extended paragraph for strings alone – a passage of some sixty bars – that arises from the 'Faustian' opening (Ex. 20a): an object lesson, this, in how to achieve an almost static, expectant effect while keeping the music in motion. Particularly impressive is the command of motive, line and tonality, and the generative power it sustains. The lyrical theme (clarinet, fig. 5) is felt to grow out of this sombre opening, and yet its character is quite distinct. This material is developed and quietly restated; only then is a third theme (second subject) introduced – a simple but strongly characterised embodiment of 'nervy' semitones (flute, fig. 17). The huge central span of the movement embraces both the main development, in which every move involves at least two of the three themes, and the first part of the recapitulation. The follow-through is absolute, and the sense of gradually curving away from the climax, though slightly modified by the return of the second subject (clarinets in thirds, fig. 57), continues into the coda, where the pace and mood of the opening are resumed – with a difference. The texture is fuller and fragments of the lyrical theme, with warm harmonic support, are poignantly recalled above 'Faustian' murmurings.

As an example of Shostakovich's ability to think in long dynamic periods, the second movement (*Allegro* – B flat minor) is perhaps still more remarkable than the central span of the first, for it depends on so much less. This is a highly concentrated *moto perpetuo* in 2/4, unsurpassed in intensity and brilliantly realised. Even here, however, there is a problem of tone. One Soviet view is that this music 'expresses again the inexhaustible forces of life'. Others, also Russian, have interpreted it as a 'black march' – 'the onslaught of the powers of darkness and death'. Certainly the sense of exhilaration is shot through with something sinister, and it is possible to feel that the music faces in two directions, the one

47

affirmative, the other menacing. The purely musical issues are closely and consistently pursued, so the explanation would seem to lie in the unrevealed programme.

The succeeding *Allegretto* (C minor) is a kind of intermezzo, almost nocturnal in character, or so it initially appears. In the main this is a dialogue between two themes, the one reflective, the other more active. The second, brighter theme, in G major, embraces Shostakovich's personal motto, DSCH (D, E flat, C, B). The dialogue is interrupted by a horn-call figure of five notes. This is heard twelve times in all – the same insistent summons, never extended – and on its first appearance heralds a wholly unexpected reference to the coda of the first movement (see figs. 115 and 65). Why this dramatically pointed reference back? Here again, almost certainly, the programme holds the answer. That this seeming intermezzo is in fact of programmatic importance is confirmed by the presence of DSCH, which becomes associated with a Tchaikovsky-like dramatic crisis. Furthermore, the beginning of the first theme (Ex. 20c) is a paraphrase of the opening of the scherzo of the (withheld) Violin Concerto, which also introduces DSCH.

When the Tenth was new, and even as late as 1959, I adversely criticised the finale as 'a brilliant summing-up which mysteriously leaves the vital issues undecided'.[1] While recognising the effect of the piece, that reaction shows a failure to perceive the imaginative idea. There *is* something unfinal here, but it is knowing and deliberate and not at all a miscalculation. This finale is in two parts, a slow *Andante* in B minor leading to an *Allegro* in E major. Beautifully scored for strings, timpani and solo woodwind, the *Andante* epitomises the inner core of sadness and unease. Both the melody (lower strings, then oboe) and the heartfelt cry which follows are redeployed in the middle of the *Allegro* (fig. 185), where they are associated with a slow, solemn statement of DSCH. Earlier (fig. 176) there is a different use of the same material: the melody (Ex. 21a, opposite) is given a skipping, *scherzando* treatment (b), and the 'cry' becomes almost panic-stricken.

However, the immediate relationship between the *Andante* and the *Allegro* is one of contrast. The new texture is fresh and youthful, and the principal theme, sparked off by that aspiring interval, the

[1] See 'Shostakovich: Some Later Works', *Tempo*, Winter number (50), 1959. This includes a more detailed discussion of Symphonies Nos. 10 and 11.

48

Ex.21

perfect fifth, has an infectious gaiety suggestive of the *buffo* tradition. Still, there is an underlying tension, which becomes more marked as the music progresses and culminates (after fig. 184) in a reference to the second movement in its more sinister aspect. When the youthful themes return, their juxtaposition is more hectic, a good deal is made of DSCH, and the symphony ends on a note of tense exuberance. The impact is affirmative but provisional: anti-pessimistic rather than optimistic. In this the divergence from the path of the Fifth does not need labouring.

Not until the Fifteenth (1971) was Shostakovich to write another purely orchestral symphony of the personal-dramatic type. The fact that the next two symphonies (Nos. 11 and 12) are based on *objective* programmes sets them apart: compare, for example, Tchaikovsky's *Manfred* in relation to his Fourth or Sixth. This does not mean that the Eleventh and the Twelfth are inherently 'less symphonic', but it does mean a different relationship between the composer and the content of his work.

Two Programme Symphonies (Nos. 11 and 12)

These two symphonies with historical programmes were written in 1957 and 1961 to mark the fortieth and forty-fourth anniversaries of the October Revolution. Of all such commemorative works by Soviet composers, and the number is now considerable, Shostakovich's Eleventh Symphony, in G minor (*The Year 1905*), Op. 103, seems likely to prove the most enduring. After the immense success achieved with this work, Shostakovich must have had many requests for a sequel based on the October Revolution itself. The Twelfth, in D minor (*The Year 1917*), Op. 112, is such a sequel. Although smaller in scale, it is built on a similar plan with four linked movements, through-thematicism and close attention to musical unity. There are no loose threads in either of these symphonies. That the Eleventh strikes the more deeply – has there been a dissenting opinion? – may be partly because it was the first, and partly because the programme engaged Shostakovich's tragic sense no less than his socialist conscience.

SYMPHONY NO. 11 IN G MINOR

At the centre of the Eleventh is the massacre of unarmed workmen in the square of the Winter Palace, St Petersburg, on 9 January 1905. In the second movement, *Ninth of January* – some 130 pages of full score – this event is depicted with graphic realism; it is like a vast mural representation, but with the immediacy and sense of conflict that only musical motion can convey. This is preceded by *Palace Square*, a bleak, introductory movement which sets the scene and evokes an atmosphere of tense, oppressive calm, shot through with hints of impending action. Again, this static sense is something that music alone – music in motion – can project on so large a scale. This is not a paradox; it is simply that suppressed or interrupted motion, which cannot escape the time-scale, is more arresting than that which is literally static (cf. the opening of the Tenth). After *Ninth of January* comes *Eternal Memory*, an elegy for the thousand and more left dead in the square by the Tsar's soldiers, and finally *The Tocsin*, an expression of revolutionary fervour.

It is evident that a great deal of careful planning went into the realisation of this scheme. The musical and the programmatic could hardly have been more closely brought together, at every level; and so the symphonic impulse emerges strongly, but without ever suggesting that the programme is a gloss or afterthought. Even in his choice of folk-song material, Shostakovich succeeded in reconciling musical function not only with mood but with the words belonging to the tunes. For instance, the sadly beautiful flute melody in *Palace Square* is from a song about a prisoner who has lost all hope, and the theme of the first part of *Ninth of January* – the gathering of workmen to petition the Tsar – is based on a folk-song whose words begin:

> Oh, Tsar, our little father!
> Look around you;
> Life is impossible for us because of the Tsar's servants,
> Against whom we are helpless . . .

The latter example affords further insights into Shostakovich's methods. Look carefully at these four bars (bars 12–15 of *Ninth of January*):

Ex.22

The upper part shows the first (crucial) phrase of the theme, of which the lower part (bar 1) is a free diminution. This urgent, restless idea on the lower strings, already established in the first eleven bars, provides the essential 'current' for this part of the movement, and it does so in a way that is closely related not only to the 'little father' theme but also to the 'motto' which is basic to the whole work:

Ex.23

This is the 'motto' as we first hear it, quietly on the timpani, very early in the opening movement. As is the nature of mottoes when they are really pervasive – compare, for example, Rachmaninov's Second Symphony – this idea is extremely simple: an insistent rhythm with conflicting minor and major thirds (C flat = B natural). Such simplicity is also effectively pliable; the idea can be manipulated freely without harm to its identity. What happens to Ex. 23 is (i) straightforward recurrence, (ii) transformation and development, and (iii) embodiment in other material, as has been shown in Ex. 22. The most striking example of transformation – or thematic derivation – also occurs in *Ninth of January*: the terse, choppy theme, marvellously apt for its purpose, first heard on the cellos and basses at the beginning of the second big *Allegro* section, the massacre itself (fig. 71). There is another telling example of (iii) at the beginning of *Eternal Memory*, where the *pizzicato* accompaniment embodies the conflicting thirds.

As well as the 'motto', other ideas from the first movement recur later on, and almost invariably these cross-references combine dramatic point with musical effectiveness. The most important is the opening string music (*Adagio* and *pp*), which is indeed closely associated with the 'motto' but memorable in its own right. One of the masterstrokes in this work, both musically and pictorially, is the way in which the tumult of the massacre suddenly ceases, leaving only that string music, now elaborated with fluttering trills. Such vital image-making within so well ordered a musical stream entitles the Eleventh to rank highly among the achievements of programme music. Of particular interest, from another point of view, is the fact that there is nowhere the slightest problem of tone.

The least impressive movement is the last. This is a march-like *moto perpetuo* which in general character may be said to stand somewhere between the finale of the Tenth and that of the Fifth. Everything is relevant and closely knit, and a sense of revolutionary fervour is not wanting; but, as Edmund Rubbra has remarked, the 'breathless energy and steely brilliance . . . tends, in the long run, to deaden one's sensibilities'.[1] The basic material is less gripping, less distinguished, and the imaginative level of *Ninth of January*, the movement with which the finale is necessarily in competition, is not really matched. In the later stages, however, the difficult and dangerous task of drawing together themes from the other

[1] *The Listener*, 18 December 1975, p. 832.

movements – *Ninth of January* figures prominently here – is accomplished with great skill and dramatic point. The last sounds we hear are the alternating minor and major thirds of the 'motto' ringing out on bells against the fullness (*fff espressivo*) of the whole orchestra. And so the work ends, not in defeat but in a vision of future victory.

SYMPHONY NO. 12 IN D MINOR

As early as 1938, in the immediate wake of his Fifth Symphony, Shostakovich had planned a large-scale composition for soloists, chorus and orchestra to be dedicated to the memory of Lenin. The plan came to nothing, and in the end his Lenin symphony proved to be his Twelfth. This is a quite different conception, closely allied to the Eleventh, and there is no reason to suppose that any of the earlier material was turned to account. Nonetheless, one wonders whether the important hymn-like melody (Ex. 24), the role of which is comparable with that of the 'motto' in the Eleventh, has any connection with the 'songs about Lenin' that Shostakovich had intended to use in 1938.

Ex.24 **Allegro**

The most obvious difference between the Eleventh and the Twelfth is one of scale. And if the Twelfth can afford to be smaller, the reason is that the programme is more generalised and the working less concerned with graphic detail. For example, there is a marked difference between the detailed scene-painting of *Palace Square* and the sonata *Allegro* which is *Revolutionary Petrograd*. Similarly, there is nothing comparable with *Ninth of January*, the dramatic core of the Eleventh. The second movement, *Razliv*, is a meditative *Adagio*. The third, '*Aurora*', is the most graphic movement but also the shortest – in effect an introduction to the finale, *The Dawn of Humanity*.

It is interesting to recall the remarks about the first movement of his Tenth Symphony which Shostakovich made in his opening statement at a three-day public discussion on the Tenth held in Moscow under the auspices of the Union of Soviet Composers, March–April 1954:

I see that I did not succeed in doing what I've dreamed of for a long time: writing a real symphonic *Allegro*. It did not come to me in this symphony, any more than it did in my previous symphonic works. But I hope that one day I shall succeed in writing such an *Allegro*. . . .

Now *Revolutionary Petrograd* is indeed 'such an *Allegro*', in D minor, and if we discount the Ninth, as Shostakovich seems to have done, the Twelfth is virtually his only symphony to begin in this way. The principal theme (bassoons) is a rhythmically animated version of the very Russian, folk-like melody of the introductory *Moderato*, and the second subject (B flat major) is the hymn-like theme already quoted (Ex. 24). The working is vigorous and well ordered with a close dovetailing of the development and recapitulation; but the overall impression is one of skilful and knowing construction rather than deep imagination. The introductory theme is heard again in both the development and the coda – and is to reappear in the finale; but it is the 'hymn' that is basic to the whole work, recurring in each of the subsequent movements.

The title of the second movement, *Razliv*, refers to the place north of Petrograd where Lenin was in hiding on the eve of the Revolution. This *Adagio* (F sharp minor), for the most part sombre and full of suppressed tension, may or may not be a portrait of Lenin alone. Musically, it is another memorable example of Shostakovich's use of musical motion to create an effect that is static, suspended, and yet charged with latent energy. Much depends on the nature of the theme heard at once on the cellos and basses:

Ex.25　**Adagio**

The chief characteristics are the broken phrase-structure and the quiet reiteration of the first phrase, which doubles back on itself and counters any tendency there may be to move forward. Much is made of both this first phrase (x) and the plucked cadence-figure (y), but always by repetition, not development. There are two references to the beginning of the hymn-like theme (Ex. 24), and after the second of these comes a new idea (flute and clarinet, pp), a theme that is to dominate '*Aurora*'. This, too, is characterised by suppressed activity, its little excursions and irregularities serving to emphasise the tight grip on the music of E flat major. Only at the close is there a return to F sharp minor.

It was ingenious to seize on the incident involving the cruiser *Aurora* as a means of representing the Revolution itself.[1] This gave rise to a single concrete image – a mounting crescendo of activity – and avoided the necessity of 'repeating' *The Tocsin*. Beginning with quiet drum-taps, '*Aurora*' is one of the most successful embodiments of Shostakovich's embattled percussion; weight and proportion are exactly right, and the impulse is musical throughout. The title of the finale, *The Dawn of Humanity*, and the presence of a theme that Shostakovich associated with 'the joys of youth' bring to mind Wordsworth on the French Revolution:

> Bliss was it in that dawn to be alive,
> But to be young was very heaven!

These two lines would make an apt superscription, and in fitness and warmth of expression the music may be felt to match them. Of great thematic importance is the forthright paean played by the horns (ff) at the beginning. This establishes the musical character and provides a framework for the triumphal return of both the 'hymn' and the introductory theme from the first movement. The triumphal note might easily have sounded shallow, brash or pompous. In fact, however, this finale is not without dignity, but it impresses by virtue of its fitness and good workmanship rather than through any deeper quality of imagination.

---

[1] The Revolution began when the *Aurora*, in the hands of a sailors' soviet, moved up from Kronstadt and shelled the Winter Palace.

Symphony No. 13 in B flat minor ('Babi Yar')

After the Eleventh and Twelfth with their programmes of revolution there was much speculation about Shostakovich's future course as a symphonist. This was heightened by the character, and quality, of other works from the same period, notably the Cello Concerto No. 1 and the String Quartets Nos. 7 and 8. The answer came surprisingly quickly: the Thirteenth Symphony, in B flat minor, for bass solo, male chorus and orchestra is Op. 113, which places it immediately after the Twelfth (*The Year 1917*). The date is 1962, at the height of 'the thaw' which followed Khrushchev's de-mythologising of Stalin; and since the text consists of poems by Yevgeny Yevtushenko, including two or three of his most outspoken, we do not need to be political detectives to see a possible point in the juxtaposition of these two symphonies. We *may* be intended to make a connection, to see the evils of Stalinism against the background of *The Dawn of Humanity*. Beyond that it is not possible to go.

The five movements are headed *Babi Yar* – commonly used as a title for the whole work, though not, it seems, by Shostakovich – *Humour, In the Store, Fears* and *A Career*, and there can be no doubt that the text amounts to a finely-pointed critique of Stalinist society. Humour is personified as one who mocks oppressive authority and 'cannot be bought'; *In the Store* celebrates the women of Russia who 'have endured everything'; *Fears* refers explicitly to 'the secret fear at someone informing, the secret fear at a knock at the door', and *A Career* is about integrity, with Galileo as the worthy example. The poem *Babi Yar* had already caught the attention of authority, and Shostakovich's use of it proved too much even for Khrushchev, who is said to have recommended, in vain, that the first performance be cancelled. This is the point at which the truth becomes hard to disentangle. It appears that a second performance was postponed because Khrushchev insisted that the text of *Babi Yar* be revised. Eventually, some changes were made; but Yevtushenko is reported as saying: 'Nobody forced me to change. I wished to expand slightly on the scope of the poem . . . I made the verse better for publication.'[1] The extent of the revision may be seen by comparing the text accompanying the HMV-Melodiya

[1] Nonetheless, at the Cheltenham Festival of Literature, 1975, Yevtushenko read what seemed to be the original version.

recording (ASD 2893, or SLS 5025) with the original in the (Canadian) published score. Two passages, each of four lines, are affected. In the first the revised version notes that at Babi Yar Ukrainians as well as Jews were massacred by the Nazis, and in the second the poet pays tribute to Russia's part in fighting Fascism. Here are the two passages – the originals are given first, in brackets:

1. [I feel myself a Jew. Here I tread across old Egypt. Here I die, nailed to the cross, and even now I bear the scars of the nails.]
   Here I stand as if at the fountainhead that gives me faith in our brotherhood. Here Russians lie, and Ukrainians lie together with the Jews in the same ground.
2. [I become a gigantic scream above the thousands buried here. I am every old man shot dead here. I am each small child shot dead here.]
   I think of Russia's heroic deed in blocking the way to Fascism. To the smallest dewdrop she is close to me with her very being and her fate.

The most significant aspect of these revisions has generally been missed: they do not touch the offending passages which imply the continued presence of anti-Semitism in official Russia.

The fate of the Thirteenth today is obscure. In the late 1960s it was commonly said that the performance in Moscow on 20 November 1965 was 'the last in Russia'. The Melodiya recording, however, dates from 1972, which would seem to suggest a better situation. The Composers' Union denies that there have been long periods when the work has not been performed and says that 'recently' it was given at Minsk; but the Soviet Music Propaganda Bureau, also in Moscow, recognises that the Thirteenth is not performed often. Whatever the truth may be, the fact that this symphony was ever obstructed, let alone banned, is heavy with tragic irony. Not the least ironic aspect is what I take to be the excellence of the music *from the Soviet point of view*. The atmosphere is strongly Russian, the musical background rich in associations, the expressive foreground clear and direct; and who is to say that this, of all Shostakovich's works, is not patriotic? – or not realistic?

It is tempting to write of the 'plainness' of the Thirteenth, but the term lacks the necessary overtones. What is involved is a blend of economy, directness and the kind of simplicity that Shostakovich himself considered ideal – see the superscription to this book. Nowhere is this quality more evident than in the choral writing: the 40–100 voices prescribed in the score sing in unison throughout. Whether stark and defiant or warm and tender, this unanimity is itself a powerful image and does much to establish the tone of the shimmering stillness, very Russian in atmosphere, is one of a number of instances of magically simple scoring – for the most part extensions of textures to be found in the Fifth. Another is at the lead-back to the opening material (fig. 28), where repeated notes on a solo horn are heard against high trills on violins and celesta and changing harmonies on the lower woodwind and string instruments.

In the brilliantly mercurial scherzo, which follows, scoring is likewise an important element. This movement is not a scherzo and trio; rather is it shaped against the background of sonata form, but in a way that is little concerned with defining any ground-plan. When the opening is recapitulated, it is with great freedom, beginning with a twofold presentation of the clarinet theme: i.e. in its original form, now played by the bass clarinet, together with an inversion on a solo flute (fig. 68). This passage with its dazzling sleight of hand exemplifies the temper of the piece. The emphasis throughout is on the stream of invention, but with close attention to continuity and to the endlessly changing internal relationships. There is a feeling that the more rewarding aspects of Shostakovich's earlier abandon are re-created here and given a more positive perspective. There is also a feeling that the tone is elusive. Although a joyful exuberance undoubtedly predominates, this is not entirely free from apparent 'sarcasms', and there are passages where Orlov's reference to 'the theme of "evil powers"' is supported. A problem arises because these different elements do not appear to be purposefully related.

There are no such problems in the *Presto* finale, where all is high spirits from first to last. This is a rondo, in B major, and perhaps Shostakovich's closest approach to Prokofiev – the Prokofiev of the Third Piano Concerto. The second strain of the principal theme shows this affinity and is representative of the whole expression, both rhythmically and melodically:

Ex.15

Ex. 26 shows (a) the root idea – a 'basic tendency' rather than a motto (cf. the String Quartet No. 9, Op. 117), (b) and (c) instances of its use in the first movement, and (d) the form in which it pervades the third and fourth movements. Together with the important opening theme (Ex. 27), this five-note figure (*x*) may be shown to bear directly on many of the thematic connections built up throughout the work.

Ex.27   **Adagio**

One's first impression of the opening is that it is a splendid example of Shostakovich's flair for evoking an atmosphere – cf. the beginning of the Eleventh. And so it is; but it is also rich in significant detail. The characteristic semiquaver figure (muted trumpets and horns) which opens outwards chromatically, each part spanning a minor third, is of far-reaching importance; the minor third itself, which links Exx. 26 and 27, is nothing if not pervasive, and the diminished fifth is another important element. That one singles out intervals rather than themes is indicative of the kind of impact this music makes. Every detail seems to have expressive power and compositional relevance. This is true of the chord- and key-relations, too, as is strikingly revealed at the beginning of the second movement (*Allegretto* – effectively the scherzo) where repeated C major triads on the woodwinds and horns are blared out against contrary elements on the strings. This introduces a view of C major that is basic to the whole expression – and a vein of humour that is Shostakovich at his most Eulenspiegel-like! Incidentally, one theme in this second movement is a self-quotation. It is the satirical tune that opens and closes *Macpherson's Farewell* (Burns), the third of the Six Romances to Verses by English Poets, Op. 62/140, and its presence here (fig. 51) springs from the thought of Humour breaking into a 'dashing dance' and going to his execution as a political prisoner – ideas that connect with the first stanza of Burns's poem.

A large orchestra is used, including triple woodwind, a sizable battery, a piano and 2–4 harps. There are indeed some wonderfully trenchant climaxes in the manner of the Eleventh or the Eighth, but the predominant impression is one of highly selective scoring, much of it very finely pointed and, in the best sense, idiosyncratic. Some of the instrumental colourings are in themselves decisive imaginative strokes: for instance, the solo tuba at the beginning of the fourth movement, and the flutes in sixths at the beginning of the fifth. And in cases such as these the listener feels that the musical idea and its presentation were always one in the mind of the composer. Similarly, much of the thematic working seems inseparable from the almost chamber-musical clarity of the textures it creates. Another striking feature is the thematic importance given to the cellos and basses. Here, perhaps, one thinks of the first movement of the Tenth, in which a dark, sonorous bass line is likewise associated with a largely conjunct thematicism.

The five-movement form with the last three movements linked together, the last of all being a wistful *Allegretto* in the tonic major with a *morendo* close, can hardly fail to prompt comparison with the Eighth. What makes such a comparison valuable is an important difference in the composer's relationship with his work. In the Eighth Shostakovich was engaged in 'solving' a personal-dramatic problem; the creative act was both a form of catharsis and a search for clarification. In the Thirteenth, surely, all was clear, emotionally and spiritually, before the notes were set down. The implications of this difference are particularly marked in the two last movements. That of the Thirteenth, far from being in any sense 'problematical', is absolutely firm in the clarity of its perception. Throughout the work this quality has much to do with that ideal simplicity already remarked on.

The Last Two Symphonies

The Thirteenth has been described as 'a symphonic cantata rather than a true symphony', but experience has shown that its claim to be a symphony can easily be underestimated. However, the next in the series may well be thought misnamed. This Fourteenth Symphony, Op. 135 (1969), is orchestral chamber music of the finest sort; it is also a memorable song-cycle – but not in any meaningful sense a symphony. Why, then, did Shostakovich so designate it? Was it to show that, if a work like the Thirteenth was to remain in limbo, he would write no further 'public' symphonies? I find this suggestion, which has been seriously argued, wholly speculative, without any supporting evidence; but it does at least draw attention to the intensely inward, personal nature of the music. Far better, I suggest, to concentrate on what the work *is* than to argue about nomenclature.

The forces used are two solo singers – a soprano and a bass – a group of ten percussion instruments and a small string orchestra. The percussion has none of its heavier members, the only drums being three tom-toms, introduced simply to meet the needs of one poem (Apollinaire's *On the Alert*). The strings intended are 10 violins, 4 violas, 3 cellos and 2 double-basses. These numbers should be considered obligatory, not least because of the extensive use of division. At one point the violins, for instance, have no fewer than ten parts, at another point eight, and passages in three or four parts are fairly common. The other strings, including the two double-basses, are also much divided. Clearly, every detail in the instrumental writing has been imagined with a truly chamber-musical precision.

Shostakovich's increasing concern with chamber music has a further bearing on this composition. In both the String Quartet No. 12, Op. 133, and the Sonata for Violin and Piano, Op. 134 – the two works immediately preceding the Fourteenth Symphony – 12-note material plays a crucial part, conditioning much of the musical character. Such material is used extensively in the Fourteenth. As in all these works, the context remains tonal, and it would be misleading, almost always, to refer loosely to the presence of 'serial technique', for that would imply something much more comprehensive and systematic than is encountered here.

Essentially, Shostakovich's use of this material is melodic, even thematic. Representative examples may be quoted from the setting already referred to – *On the Alert*, which is no. 5 in the cycle.

Ex.28

The xylophone refrain (Ex. 28a), first heard at the beginning, is a 12-note theme in which perfect fourths and fifths, far from being avoided because of their tonal implications, are actively embraced. The *pizzicato* string passage (Ex. 28b), which answers the first entry of the soprano, typifies the more general melodic use of 12-note material. Here, too, the intervals are worth pondering; and notice the effect of the repeated C. The language of the Fourteenth, though highly concentrated, leaves the composer free to be as chromatic or as diatonic as he chooses, and the impact of the work is closely bound up with Shostakovich's superb control over the immense range of tensions at his disposal.

The dedication is to Benjamin Britten, with whose *Nocturne* for tenor, seven obbligato instruments and strings the basic conception has much in common. There are no linking passages in the manner of the *Nocturne*, but most of the eleven songs are joined together and the overall effect is continuous. Just as Britten's subject is sleep, so Shostakovich's is death, and his choice of texts is a very personal one. At the centre is a group of six peoms by Apollinaire; at the beginning there are two by Lorca, and the cycle is completed with one by Küchelbecker – the only Russian represented – and two by Rilke:

1. *De Profundis* (Lorca) – bass, with violins, violas and double-basses only.
2. *Malagueña* (Lorca) – soprano.
3. *Lorelei* (Apollinaire) – soprano and bass.
4. *The Suicide* (Apollinaire) – soprano.
5. *On the Alert* (Apollinaire) – soprano.
6. *Madam, Look!* (Apollinaire) – soprano and bass.
7. *At the Santé Jail* (Apollinaire) – bass.
8. *The Zaporozhian Cossacks' Reply to the Sultan of Constantinople* (Apollinaire) – bass, with strings only.
9. *O Delvig, Delvig!* (Küchelbecker) – bass, with strings only.
10. *The Death of a Poet* (Rilke) – soprano.
11. *Conclusion* (Rilke) – soprano and bass.

This anthology of death ranges widely in expression, from the macabre and ironic *Malagueña* and the dramatic *scena* that is *Lorelei* to the various qualities of inwardness revealed by *At the Santé Jail* (sometimes known as *In Prison*), *O Delvig, Delvig!* and *The Death of a Poet*. One of the most memorable is *The Suicide,* which shows once again that in his response to suffering and misfortune Shostakovich is the only true successor to Mussorgsky. All, however, are intensely felt and precisely imagined. One further point of contrast with the preceding symphonies – as striking as the unsymphonic form – is the absence of a through-thematicism. The only thematic cross-reference is between no. 1 and no. 10. These two songs begin with the same unaccompanied violin theme, the effect of which is to place nos. 1–10 within a frame and to give the brief but shattering no. 11 the function of an epilogue. No less than in the Thirteenth, the word-setting is syllabic, without a trace of flourishes or embellishments. Every interval and note-value is felt to spring from the natural movement of the words, but in a way that is highly sensitive to inflexions and shades of emphasis. The voice parts are always 'grateful' from the singers' point of view, and they show very clearly the strength of Shostakovich's commitment to tonality.

SYMPHONY NO. 15 IN A MAJOR

The Fifteenth Symphony, Op. 141 (1971), brings a return to the purely orchestral symphony in four movements. Apart from a large percussion section, which includes almost all the percussion instruments used in the Fourteenth, and a number of others, the orchestral requirements are comparatively modest for Shostakovich but otherwise unremarkable. Even so, it is doubtful whether any useful comparison can be made with the earlier sequence of personal-dramatic symphonies (Nos. 5–10), let alone the Eleventh and Twelfth, for the musical presence – and, surely, the creative approach – seems to set the work apart. This is not to suggest that the Fifteenth was knowingly planned as a 'last symphony'.[1] Nor is it to deny the extraordinary richness of personal fingerprints. There are, I think, three important features that contribute to the uniqueness of character: the nature of the scoring, the range of the material, and the use of quotations and apparent allusions. Each of these calls for comment.

The listener's first impression, apart from fingerprints, is of the freshness and openness of the orchestral sound. The more densely scored passages, such as the climaxes of the slow movement and the finale, stand out as rare exceptions, the number of bars of tutti being a minute proportion of the whole. Soloistic and chamber-musical qualities of scoring have been remarked on in a number of these symphonies, but in the Fifteenth such qualities are all-pervasive. They sharpen the wit and heighten the pathos. Moreover, the prevailing clarity, or selectivity, gives the music a peculiar directness.

The material extends from the simplest of diatonic tunes – jingles, almost – to various kinds of expression using all twelve notes. The two extremes not only coexist; they interact and interpenetrate, creating an enlarged tonal field in which 'chromatic' and 'diatonic' cease to be meaningful distinctions. This may be readily perceived in the opening *Allegretto* – a teasing, witty piece, relaxed and yet needle-sharp. The principal 'second subject' idea (Ex. 29, opposite) illustrates with disarming simplicity Shostakovich's way of harnessing the twelve semitones. And a comparison with Ex. 17 (see p. 40) will tend to support the view that this is a natural extension of an established style. Whatever else it may be, this opening movement is a brilliant demonstration of the composer's flair for semitonal side-steps and the mobility to be attained with them. It follows that there is nothing magical about the number 12; 11- and 10-note ideas, similar in feeling, are also to be found.

The quotations are from Rossini and Wagner. In the first movement a familiar snatch of the *William Tell* overture is heard five times, always in the key of the home dominant (E major). This is closely associated with the theme shown in Ex. 29, and at one

[1] At the time of his death Shostakovich had a new symphony in progress.

Ex.29

point (fig. 26) the two are heard simultaneously. Why *William Tell*? It appears that the sleeve-note for the original Russian recording 'placed' this movement in a toyshop at night: the toys come to life, and the quotation represents a toy soldier. Is this the real meaning or a subsequent gloss? A little scepticism seems reasonable, for in its context the Rossini sounds like a musical snook, however genial, and the atmosphere is hardly nocturnal.

The Wagner poses a deeper problem, for this threefold quotation introduces the finale and is itself already heavy with meaning. First we hear the Fate motive from *The Ring* (horns and trombones), followed at once by the rhythm of Siegfried's Funeral Music, also known as the Death motive (timpani). When these have been repeated, the first violins lead into an *Allegretto* of childlike freshness – but with the first three notes of the *Tristan* prelude! These cryptic 'sayings' insist on being interpreted. But how? Eugene Ormandy sees the finale as 'a musical canvas that could be entitled "They Shall Not Be Forgotten"': i.e. a further memorial to Russia's wartime dead, with the Wagner strains perhaps 'a gesture of reconciliation'.[1] There would seem to be support for such a view in the middle of the movement where a passacaglia is built up to a

[1] See the sleeve of Ormandy's recording with the Philadelphia Orchestra (RCA ARD1–0014).

harrowing climax over a ground bass fourteen bars long. The first four bars of the passacaglia theme (Ex. 30a) appear to be an allusion to the beginning of the War theme in the *Leningrad* Symphony (b).

Ex.30

If these findings are correct, what is the connection with the toy shop at night? Does the prominence given to the toy soldier have some hidden significance? Or is it mistaken to assume the existence of a comprehensive programme?

Further questions are raised by the three unmistakable references to the percussion pattern at the end of the second movement of the Fourth Symphony. Two of these occur in the third movement, which also contains a single (transposed) statement of the DSCH motive familiar from the Tenth Symphony and other works (horns against a trombone *glissando* – six bars after fig. 92). The other reference to the percussion pattern is at the very end of the symphony, where it is heard against the bare fifth A–E sustained throughout the strings, and in company with quiet reminders of the passacaglia theme (timpani and xylophone). The flute motive from the opening bars of the symphony is also recalled at this point (celesta and piccolo).

Does the Fifteenth contain any other allusions to Shostakovich's previous works? Given the profusion of fingerprints, it is not surprising that several possibilities have been suggested. None of these, however, is firmly based. For instance, to cite the opening as a reference to the First Cello Concerto shows excessive enthusiasm; the two ideas, though of a similar nature, are quite distinct.

The problems of meaning remain and are, perhaps, reinforced by the seemingly loose association of the four movements – and, indeed, by the ambiguous tone of the first and third movements. In both, different as they are, the basic character might be described as *scherzando*. The first, at least to begin with, is outwardly an expression of gaiety and high spirits, but one comes to suspect an underlying irony. The third, another *Allegretto*, is one of the supreme examples of that poker-faced quality which has been remarked on in these pages several times, and which so often seems to mask sardonic intentions. In between these movements comes a deeply disturbing *Adagio* in F minor, of which the sombre opening (brass) may be felt to foreshadow the Wagner Fate motive. The important cello solo, which follows at once, carries the main elegiac burden – and, incidentally, provides a further memorable example of Shostakovich's 12-note melodic writing (from fig. 53). By comparison, the subsequent trombone solo sounds curiously artless, in a way that can only have been deliberate. Once again the listener is virtually prodded into asking what the composer had in mind.

Those whose musical instinct is to reject such questions may well consider the Fifteenth one of the most straightforward of Shostakovich's major works. Each musical step is beautifully clear, nowhere is there a note too many, and the scoring is lucidity itself. Paradoxically, this is also the most enigmatic of the symphonies, the one in which the underlying thought seems most to be withheld. And so it takes its place with the last string quartets as an essentially 'private' composition, but one in which public concerns may well be deeply embedded.

Index